How Artists View Food

Karen Hosack

Heinemann Library
Chicago, Illinois

Designed by Ron Kamen and Celia Floyd
Illustrations by Jo Brooker
Originated by Dot Gradations Ltd
Printed and bound in China by South China Printing Company

09 08 07 06 05
10 9 8 7 6 5 4 3 2 1

Library of Congress Cataloging-in-Publication Data

Hosack, Karen.
  Food / Karen Hosack.
    v. cm. -- (How artists view)
  Includes index.
  Contents: How artists see food -- Patterns and food -- Good enough to eat! -- Textures of food -- Food and meaning -- Arranging food -- Harvest time -- Displaying food -- Supper time! -- Food sculpture -- Strange uses of food -- You are what you eat -- Zoom in close.
  ISBN 1-4034-4852-3
  1. Food in art--Juvenile literature. 2. Art--Juvenile literature. [1. Food in art. 2. Art appreciation.] I. Title. II. Series.
  N8217.F64H67 2004
  704.9'496413--dc22
                                    2003026349

Acknowledgments

The author and publisher are grateful to the following for permission to reproduce copyright material:

Alamy p. 28 (Harrison Smith); Amsterdam Rijksmuseum p. 20; Art Institute of Chicago p. 15; Bridgeman Art Library pp. 4 (The Andy Warhol Foundation for the Visual Arts, Inc./DACS, London, 2004. Trademarks Licensed by Campbell Soup Company. All Rights Reserved.), 10 (The National Gallery, London), 14 (Collection Lillie P. Bliss, Museum of Modern Art, New York), 24 (© ADAGP, Paris and DACS, London 2004); Cameron Watt p. 18; Claes Oldenburg & Coosje van Bruggen p. 25; Corbis pp. 7 (Geoffrey Clements), 22 (John R. Jones/Papilio), 27 (Swim Ink); Edward Weston Archive p. 26; Mary Evans Picture Library p. 5; National Gallery, London pp. 12, 13, 19; Ohara Museum of Art, Japan p. 8 (© Yoshiharu Yasui & JAA, 2004); Scala, Florence pp. 16 (Louvre, Paris, 1990), 21 top (S. Maria della Grazie, Milan, 2002), 21 bottom (Rossano Cathedral, Italy, 1990); Sheldon Memorial Art Gallery and Sculpture Garden, University of Nebraska-Lincoln p. 11; Statens Museum for Kunst, Copenhagen p. 6 (© Succession H Matisse/DACS 2004); Tudor Photography pp. 9 x 3, 17 x 3, 23 x 3, 29.

Cover photograph (*Gateaux* by Philip Le Bas) reproduced with permission of Portal Gallery, London/Bridgeman Art Library.

Every effort has been made to contact copyright holders of any material reproduced in this book. Any omissions will be rectified in subsequent printings if notice is given to the publisher.

Some words are shown in bold, **like this.** You can find out what they mean by looking in the glossary.

Contents

How Artists See Food 4

Patterns and Food 6

Good Enough to Eat! 8

Textures of Food 10

Food and Meaning 12

Arranging Food 14

Harvest Time .16

Displaying Food 18

Dinner Time! 20

Food Sculpture 22

Strange Uses of Food 24

You Are What You Eat 26

Zoom in Close 28

Glossary 30

More Books to Read 31

Index 32

How Artists See Food

Food is very important in all our lives. We need food to grow and stay healthy. We also use food to celebrate special occasions like birthdays, weddings, and festivals.

Artists sometimes show food in their work. Andy Warhol's soup can is very famous. It was an everyday object the artist copied and used in his art.

Campbell's Soup Can by Andy Warhol, 1964

This **illustration** was made more than 400 years
earlier than the soup can on page 4. In the **sixteenth
century,** everyday objects in a kitchen would have
been cooking pots over a fire or baskets of
vegetables, not cans of soup!

Patterns and Food

Here, Henri Matisse has painted some onions and jugs placed on a table. He was interested in the basic shapes made by the objects. The lines of the sprouting onions and the decoration on the jugs create a strong overall sense of pattern.

Pink Onions by Henri Matisse, 1906

Cubist Still-life with Apple by Roy
Lichenstein, around 1974

This **still life** by Roy Lichenstein has two different
patterns. One pattern looks like wood grain, the
other pattern is dotty. The patterns are separated by
thick black lines that make shapes. Some of these are
fruit shapes. Can you see the apple and lemon?

Good Enough to Eat!

Grapes by Sotaro Yasui, 1952–1953

Artists use **tone** to make objects look real. In this painting, Sotaro Yasui has used different shades of the same color to make the grapes look **three-dimensional.** He has used dark shades to show the shadows, and lighter shades to show the places where the light has caught the surface of the grapes. The lighter shades are called **highlights.**

Did you know?
There is a legend about an ancient Greek artist who painted grapes so beautifully that birds flew in through the window of his studio and started pecking at them!

8

Paint your own fruit picture using tone

You will need:

- *a piece of fruit*
- *paint (any paint will do, for example watercolors or powder paint)*
- *a **palette** to mix paint on*
- *a paintbrush*
- *thick paper to paint on*

Instructions:

1. Choose a piece of fruit as your **subject,** then place it on a surface next to a window.

2. Mix three different shades of the same color on your palette. Use the medium shade to sketch the main shapes of your fruit.

3. Paint in the tones using the darkest shade for the shadows and the lightest shade for the highlights. You should now have your finished fruit painting!

Textures of Food

The objects in this **still life** were chosen for their different **textures.** Artists try to show how objects might feel if we could touch them. For example, the lobster looks hard and shiny. The lemon's flesh seems juicy and its skin waxy. The liquid in the glasses sparkles. Painting different textures is a good way for an artist to show off his or her skills.

Still Life with the Drinking-Horn of the Saint Sebastian Archers' Guild, Lobster and Glasses by Willem Kalf, around 1653

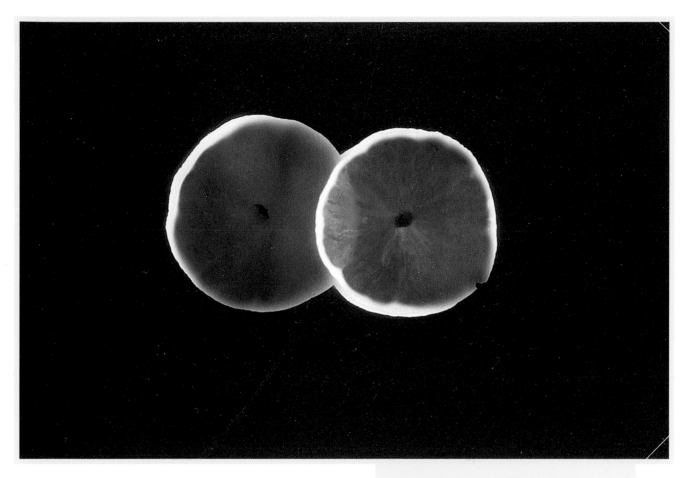

L is for Lemon Slices by
Robert Heinecken, 1971

This **photogram** allows us to see the beautiful
patterns made by the flesh of a lemon. The image
was made by placing **photograph negatives** on
top of each other.

Food and Meaning

In this painting, the artist has shown many fruits and other food. There are also lots of flowers. In the **eighteenth century,** travelers brought back food and flowers from other countries and tried to grow them at home. A lot of the food shown in this painting would have been very rare and expensive.

Fruit, Flowers and a Fish by Jan van Os, 1772

Look at this enlargement of the bottom of the painting on page twelve. There is a mouse chewing on a nut! Can you see any other animals eating their way through the food in this painting? The animals are there to remind us that unless the food is eaten, it will rot away.

Arranging Food

The way that artists place objects in a picture is called **composition.** For this painting, Cézanne arranged the apples, jug, and cup on a rumpled tablecloth. The cloth takes the viewer's eye from one object to another. We say that the cloth "ties" all the objects together in the composition.

Still Life with Apples, Cup and Pitcher
by Paul Cézanne, 1890–1900

Still Life with Game Fowl by Juan Sánchez Cotán, around 1600

Juan Sánchez Cotán painted this **still life** in a rectangular box shape. He placed some objects on the floor and hung others from the ceiling. The birds are displayed in a similar way to a butcher's shop window. The melon has been cut into slices so that we can see the inside as well as the outside.

Harvest Time

Giuseppe Arcimboldo wanted to celebrate **harvest** time by showing food gathered in late summer. He arranged fruit and vegetables in the shape of a cheerful face. Look at the round blushing cheeks and the plump smiling eyes. How many different types of food can you see?

Summer by Giuseppe Arcimboldo, around 1573

Make your own food collage self-portrait

You will need:

- *old magazines, with pictures of food*
- *scissors*
- *glue*
- *a pencil and some paper*

Instructions:

1. Find some pictures of food in old magazines and cut them out. You will use these to make your **collage.**

2. Using a sheet of paper and a pencil, make a simple outline of your face, including your mouth, nose, eyes, eyebrows, and ears.

3. Match up the food pictures with different parts of your face, and glue the pictures in place. You should now have your finished collage **self-portrait!**

1.

2.

3.

pie

cake

pie

chili

leek

Displaying Food

This photograph of food is designed to make our mouths water. Look at how the chocolate glistens and the ice cream is freshly scooped. Food stylists arrange food like this to be photographed for advertisements and cookbooks. They sometimes put paint or wax on the food to make it look even more delicious.

This painting shows a very busy market in the **sixteenth century.** The artist has shown the **textures** and colors made by the different fruits and vegetables. Some are round and shiny, like the cherries. Others are flat and rough, like the cabbage leaves. All the food at the market has been freshly picked. People did not have fridges and freezers in those days, so they had to shop for fresh food everyday.

The Four Elements: Earth by Joachim Beuckelaer, around 1570

Dinner Time!

Johannes Vermeer liked to paint everyday people doing everyday things. This Dutch woman is preparing a plain meal of bread and milk. Vermeer has used small dabs of white and yellow oil paint to show how the light through the window shines on the food and the woman's face.

The Milkmaid by Johannes Vermeer, around 1657–1658

Frescos are pictures painted straight onto **plaster** walls. This fresco by Leonardo da Vinci tells the story of the Last Supper from the Christian **Bible,** where Jesus eats with his followers for the last time. The painting covers one whole wall of a dining room in a monastery.

Last Supper by Leonardo da Vinci, around 1495–1497

Spot the difference

This sixth-century picture also shows the Last Supper. It was painted about 900 years before Leonardo da Vinci's fresco. How many differences can you see between the paintings?

Food Sculpture

A Buddhist food sculpture, made from butter

At the beginning of their new year, **Buddhists** in Tibet make **sculptures** out of butter. Traditionally they sculpt flowers, temple shapes, and figures. These are displayed in shrines and in people's homes. The sculptures soon melt in the warm weather. The melting butter stands for how quickly time passes.

Make your own food sculptures

You will need:

- *a tube of sugar cookie dough*
- *a selection of different colored food dyes*
- *a mixing bowl*

Instructions:

1. Break your dough into many small pieces. Next, use a mixing bowl to mix each piece with a few drops of food dye until the dough changes color. Use as many different food dyes as you can to color your pieces of dough. This way you will have lots of different colors of dough to build your sculptures with.

2. When you have finished coloring your pieces of dough, roll each piece into a ball. You could also roll the pieces into different shapes—it is up to you!

3. When you have done this, mix the pieces of dough together to make your finished sculptures. How many different shapes can you make?

Strange Uses of Food

This is a very odd picture. The man seems to have an apple stuck on the end of his nose! It was painted by an artist named René Magritte. He belonged to a group of artists who liked putting strange objects together in their work. This group of artists were known as **Surrealists.**

The Son of Man by René Magritte, 1964

Dropped Cone by Claes Oldenburg
and Coosje van Bruggen, 2001

This upside-down ice cream cone is huge. The artists
have placed it on a building in the middle of a busy
city. It looks like the cone has fallen out of the sky.
The ice cream even melts down the side of the
building! It is not really made out of ice-cream though.
It is a **sculpture** made from painted **fiberglass.**

You Are What You Eat

Have you ever found a piece of fruit or a vegetable that looks like something else? This pepper looks like the back of a person sitting down. It has been photographed carefully so that the light shines off the "backbone" and the "shoulders."

Pepper by Edward Weston, 1930

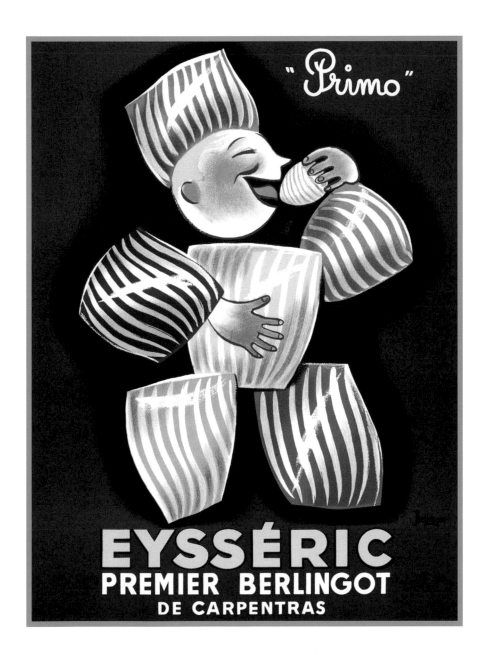

This is an advertisement. It shows a man made out of candy, eating more candy. Does it make you want to buy some? Can you think of any more advertisements that show people made out of food?

Zoom in Close

Some artists look at the shapes made by ordinary objects. This fork would normally be used to eat food. It looks more interesting if we just concentrate on its shape, rather than what it is used for. By zooming in close on everyday objects, sometimes we cannot even tell what they are at first.

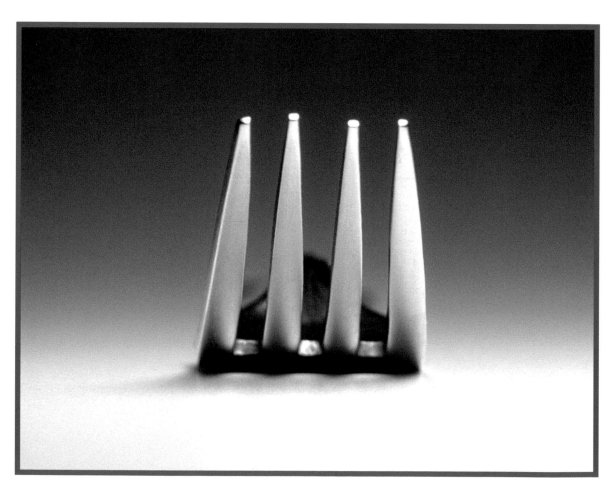

Make your own zoom-in drawing

You will need:

- *some items of food to draw, as well as some other kitchen objects like spoons or a whisk*
- *a pencil*
- *some paper*
- *a magnifying glass*

Instructions:

1. Choose an object to draw.
2. Make three or four drawings of the same object, each time getting closer and closer. You could use a magnifying glass to help you with this.
3. Show your zoom-in pictures to a friend and see if they can guess what the object is.

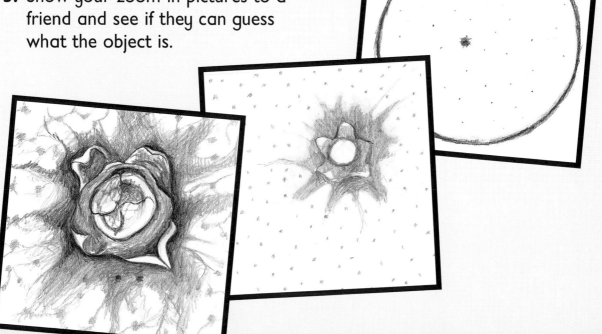

Glossary

Bible book of the Christian religion

Buddhist person who believes in the religious teachings of Buddha

collage artwork made from materials glued on to a backing

composition how a painting is put together

eighteenth century period of 100 years, from 1700 to 1799

fiberglass plastic material containing glass fibers

fresco picture painted on a plaster wall or ceiling

harvest when farmers gather their crops

highlight area in a painting that shows where light is falling

illustration drawing or picture in a book

inspire encourage someone to do something

palette tool used by artists to mix paint on

photograph negative film from a camera that can be used to make photographs

photogram picture produced using photographic paper

plaster fine white powder that sets hard when it is mixed with water and then left to dry

sculpture piece of art made from a solid material

self-portrait artist's picture of himself or herself

sixteenth century period of 100 years, from 1500 to 1599

still life picture of several objects that have been arranged in a certain way

subject person or thing in a painting or drawing

Surrealist one of a group of twentieth-century artists who explored dreams in their art

texture in art, if you give something texture, you make it look how it might feel if you could touch it

three-dimensional when an object has height, width, and depth

tone light and shade

More Books to Read

Heinemann Library's **How Artists Use** series:

- *Color*
- *Line and Tone*
- *Pattern and Texture*
- *Perspective*
- *Shape*

Heinemann Library's **The Life and Work of** series:

- *Alexander Calder*
- *Auguste Rodin*
- *Buonarroti Michelangelo*
- *Claude Monet*
- *Diego Rivera*
- *Edgar Degas*
- *Frederick Remington*
- *Georges Seurat*
- *Grandma Moses*
- *Henri Matisse*
- *Henry Moore*
- *Joseph Turner*
- *Leonardo da Vinci*
- *Mary Cassatt*
- *Paul Cezanne*
- *Paul Gauguin*
- *Paul Klee*
- *Pieter Brueghel*
- *Rembrandt van Rijn*
- *Vincent van Gogh*
- *Wassily Kandinsky*

Index

advertisements 18, 27
Arcimboldo, Giuseppe 16

Beuckelaer, Joachim 19
birds 15
Bruggen, Coosje van 25
Buddhists 22
butter sculptures 22

celebrations and festivals 4
Cézanne, Paul 14
close-up pictures 28–29
collage 17
composition 14–15
cookbooks 18
cookie dough sculptures 23
Cotán, Juan Sánchez 15

dinner 20–21
displaying food 18–19

eighteenth century 12
everyday objects 4, 5, 20, 28

fiberglass 25
food stylists 18
frescos 21
fruit 7, 8–9, 10, 11, 14, 15, 16, 19, 26

harvest time 16
Heinecken, Robert 11
highlights 8, 9

ice cream 18, 25
illustrations 5

Kalf, Willem 10

Leonardo da Vinci 21
Lichtenstein, Roy 7

Magritte, René 24
markets 19
Matisse, Henri 6
meaning of food 12
Messiburgo 5

Oldenburg, Claes 25
Os, Jan van 12

patterns 6–7
people made out of food 26–27
photograms 11
photograph negatives 11

rare and valuable food 12

sculptures 22–23, 25
shadows 8, 9
shapes 6, 7, 28
sixteenth century 5, 19
still life 7, 10, 15
strange uses of food 24–25
Surrealists 24

textures 10–11, 19
three-dimensional objects 8
tone 8, 9

vegetables 6, 16, 19, 26
Vermeer, Johannes 20

Warhol, Andy 4
Weston, Edward 26

Yasui, Sotaro 8